Remembering
Charlotte

Ryan L. Sumner

TURNER
PUBLISHING COMPANY

Looking across Charlotte's cityscape.

Remembering
Charlotte

Turner Publishing Company
www.turnerpublishing.com

Remembering Charlotte

Copyright © 2010 Turner Publishing Company

Library of Congress Control Number: 2010902292

ISBN: 978-1-59652-618-1

Printed in the United States of America

ISBN: 978-1-68336-813-7 (pbk.)

CONTENTS

Cedric "Cornbread" Maxwell led the University of North Carolina at Charlotte 49ers to victory in the NIT tournament in 1976 and to the NCAA Final Four in 1977. Maxwell was picked number 12 in the 1977 NBA draft by the Boston Celtics, for whom he played for 8 of his 11 years as a professional.

Acknowledgments

This volume, *Remembering Charlotte,* is the result of the cooperation and efforts of many individuals and organizations. It is with great thanks that we acknowledge the valuable contribution of the following for their generous support:

Mary Boyer
Carolinas Aviation Commission
Duke Energy
Federal Reserve
J. Murrey Atkins Library
Levine Museum of the New South
North Carolina State Archives
Public Library of Charlotte in Mecklenburg
University of North Carolina at Charlotte Archives

We would also like to thank Robin Brabham and Shelia Bumgarnerfor valuable contributions and assistance in making this work possible.

PREFACE

Charlotte has thousands of historic photographs that reside in archives, both locally and nationally. This book began with the observation that, while those photographs are of great interest to many, they are not easily accessible. During a time when Charlotte is looking ahead and evaluating its future course, many people are asking, How do we treat the past? These decisions affect every aspect of the city—architecture, public spaces, commerce, infrastructure—and these, in turn, affect the way that people live their lives. This book seeks to provide easy access to a valuable, objective look into the history of Charlotte.

The power of photographs is that they are less subjective than words in their treatment of history. Although the photographer can make subjective decisions regarding subject matter and how to capture and present it, photographs seldom interpret the past to the extent textual histories can. For this reason, photography is uniquely positioned to offer an original, untainted look at the past, allowing the viewer to learn for himself what the world was like a century or more ago.

This project represents countless hours of review and research. The researchers and writer have reviewed thousands of photographs in numerous archives. We greatly appreciate the generous assistance of the individuals and organizations listed in the acknowledgments of this work, without whom this project could not have been completed.

The goal in publishing this work is to provide broader access to this set of extraordinary photographs that seek to inspire, provide perspective, and evoke insight that might assist people who are responsible for determining Charlotte's future. In addition, the book seeks to preserve the past with adequate respect and reverence.

With the exception of touching up imperfections that have accrued with the passage of time and cropping where necessary, no changes have been made. The focus and clarity of many images are limited to the technology and the ability of the photographer at the time they were recorded.

The work is divided generally into eras. In each of these sections we have made an effort to capture various aspects of life through our selection of photographs. People, commerce, transportation, infrastructure, religious institutions, and educational institutions have been included to provide a broad perspective.

We encourage readers to reflect as they go walking in Charlotte, strolling through the city, its parks, and its neighborhoods. It is the publisher's hope that in utilizing this work, longtime residents will learn something new and that new residents will gain a perspective on where Charlotte has been, so that each can contribute to its future.

—*Todd Bottorff, Publisher*

A trolley plies the route in downtown Charlotte.

THE BIRTH OF A TEXTILE TYCOON

Hezekiah Alexander was a prominent farmer and one of Mecklenburg County's foremost patriots during the Revolution. Alexander held several offices in the Revolutionary government and is said to have been one of the signers of the Mecklenburg Declaration of Independence. Alexander's house, built in 1774, still stands off Shamrock Road and is cared for by the Charlotte Museum of History.

A doctor's daughter raised just north of Charlotte near Cornelius, Annie Alexander studied medicine in Philadelphia and New York. The only woman among the 100 physicians certified by the Maryland Board of Medical Examiners in 1885, she received the highest scores. The first woman licensed to practice medicine in the South, Dr. Alexander opened her office in Charlotte two years later. At first people scoffed, and she earned just $2 her first year. She persevered and quickly gained acclaim, serving at both Presbyterian and Saint Peter's hospitals, as physician for Presbyterian College, and at Camp Greene as acting assistant surgeon. Later Dr. Alexander won election to the presidency of the Mecklenburg Medical Association.

Railroad connections transformed Charlotte from just another backcountry town to a city of regional importance. In 1852, local merchants and planters built the very first railroad into the Carolina piedmont: the Charlotte and South Carolina Railroad. Rail lines continued to grow, and in 1884 several small companies joined together to form the Southern Railway—connecting Washington, D.C., to New Orleans, with Charlotte poised right in the center. Pictured is the Charlotte railroad yard (ca. 1895).

The steam fire engine of Charlotte's Company Number Seven.

Independence Square, looking northwest.

A small store at the corner of East Trade and Brevard streets (ca. 1890).

The Buford Hotel, at Fourth and South Tryon streets, was undoubtedly the finest of Charlotte's early hotels. It served as home to industrialist D. A. Tompkins, hosted prominent visitors such as Thomas Edison, and was one of the swankiest places to eat in town. In 1908, the hotel became the first headquarters of Union National Bank—which later evolved into First Union and eventually Wachovia.

Built in the 1840s at the southeast corner of Trade and Tryon streets, the Mansion was Charlotte's first stately hotel. Later called the Central Hotel, the establishment's grand ballroom hosted many lavish occasions and town dances. The grand four-story yellow-brick structure fell to the wrecking ball in the 1930s.

Tryon Street facing north, around 1900.

Big Business Takes the Stage

The 1911 graduating class of Charlotte University School—a college preparatory academy for boys founded in 1907 and owned and operated by Professor Hiram W. Glasgow. The institution closed in 1930.

Constructing roads through Myer's Park (ca. 1911). Planned by John Nolen—one of the country's best planners—this stately Charlotte neighborhood was formerly the farm of Jack S. Myers.

In 1896, Mecklenburg County erected a new courthouse at the southeast corner of Tryon and Third streets on the former site of Liberty Hall, a Revolutionary War–era academy.

Black ex-slaves had no money at the Civil War's end. Farming was the only life most had known, so they made rental agreements to borrow land, seed, tools, and mules for plowing. The owners of the land insisted that cotton be grown as a cash crop. By 1890, three-quarters of the area's African-American farmers were tenants farming someone else's land. Shown here are Mecklenburg County tenant farmers (ca. 1900).

The 1898 annual celebration of "Meck Dec Day," commemorating the alleged signing of the Mecklenburg Declaration of Independence on May 20, 1775, was one of the grandest in the history of the city—eclipsing even the Centennial Celebration. The day's ceremonies included the dedication of this monument, erected in front of the courthouse on South Tryon and East Third streets. When the county constructed a new courthouse on East Trade Street 25 years later, the obelisk was moved to the esplanade in front of the new building.

Elizabeth College, located at the intersection of Elizabeth Avenue and Hawthorne Lane, opened in 1897 for the instruction of young women. In addition to academic courses, Elizabeth offered conservatory training in art, voice, piano, and violin. The school moved to Salem, Virginia, and the grounds were acquired by Presbyterian Hospital in 1918.

The grounds of Queens College as they appeared in the early 1920s.

Trucking cotton on the old city platform (1906).

Thomas B. Hoover sits in one of his horse-drawn buggies in 1905. His livery stable stood in the 200 block of East Trade Street.

The second floor of this building served as Presbyterian Hospital's first home. Patients and nurses stand on the balcony to watch the annual Mecklenburg Declaration Day parade. Seen here about 1900, it stood on the corner of Church and Trade streets across from the Selwyn Hotel.

Located at Tryon and Fifth streets, the J. B. Ivey Company opened in May 1924. The building, designed by William Peeps at a cost of $1,250,000, is today used for shops and condominiums.

The Bee Hive—a posh dry goods, clothing, shoes, and millinery store—stood at the intersection of College and East Trade streets (ca. 1904).

Facing east down turn-of-the-century Trade Street, with the Belk Brothers department store at left.

Formed by the merger of two smaller congregations, the First Methodist Church opened its doors in 1927. Times got tough quickly, and the new congregation barely held on to its new $900,000 sanctuary during the Great Depression, finally clearing its indebtedness in 1944.

Mayor Kirkpatrick and Governor Locke Craig (ca. 1916).

President Woodrow Wilson was the guest of honor at the 1916 annual celebration of the Mecklenburg Declaration of Independence—"Meck Dec Day."

Still smarting from the loss of the Civil War and struggling against persistent poverty, business leaders organized the Charlotte Chamber of Commerce in 1877. They published "booster booklets" and advertised in magazines—anything to attract businesses to the city. Their motto, adopted in 1905, "Watch Charlotte Grow," is emblazoned on this parade drum of the Charlotte Drum Corps.

Two women park their horse and buggy in front of the Selwyn Hotel's Church Street entrance (ca. 1905).

North Tryon Street in the early years of the twentieth century. City Hall and the new Carnegie Library are at left. The steeple of First Presbyterian is visible through the trees at right.

Charlotte's U.S. Post Office when it stood on Mint Street in the early 1910s.

West Trade Street, seen from its intersection at Tryon Street (ca. 1904).

Local farmers bring their crop to market (ca. 1900).

A sea of cotton bales outside the compress (ca. 1900).

W. A. Frye and Dock Crowell opened Charlotte's first Ford garage at 221 North College Street, seen here around 1913.

Interior of the Mecklenburg Auto Company.

The Mecklenburg Auto Company at 211 South Church Street (ca. 1911). T. E. James was the president.

The city erected this new City Hall in 1891 on the southeast corner of Tryon and Fifth streets.

The Charlotte Fire Department located behind Charlotte's City Hall (January 1916).

In Charlotte, as in other southern cities, a "Black Main Street" developed near the heart of town but was set off from the official Main Street. Black businesses here clustered along East Second and spilled onto South Boulevard and McDowell streets. This area, known as "Brooklyn," became the largest of the city's half-dozen or so African-American neighborhoods. Shown here are pedestrians in the vicinity of Sanders Drugstore (ca. 1908).

Area cotton farmers bring their crop to downtown (1900).

The small building with the "Shoes" sign was Belk's first Charlotte store, which opened in 1885. Here employees pose for a photo outside the greatly expanded store on East Trade Street (ca. 1915). The store was demolished in the 1980s to make way for the Founder's Hall complex.

A horse and buggy pause for this 1905 photograph on Central Avenue in front of the home of Charles Parker—the operator of the Parker-Gardner Music Store.

South Tryon's Trust Building was the home of Catawba Power and Light as well as Charlotte's Academy of Music. Fire consumed the structure on December 17, 1922.

Picking cotton outside Charlotte.

Established as a freedman's school after the Civil War, Biddle Memorial Institute was later renamed
Biddle University and occupied this building beginning in 1883. In 1923, the school's name became
Johnson C. Smith University, and the historic administration building is now known as Biddle
Memorial Hall.

The campus of Biddle University, later renamed Johnson C. Smith University.

The Dilworth Methodist Church on East Boulevard became the congregation's home in 1926.

In 1887, Saint Peter's Episcopal Church established the Thompson Orphanage for children ages 2 through 18, becoming the first orphanage in the state supported by a religious body. The orphanage consisted of cottages, a chapel (erected in 1892), and a farm where the children and teachers milked cows. The organization moved in 1970. Only the chapel stands today, near Central Piedmont Community College.

Charlotte became the gold-trading center for the region. In March 1835, Congress approved the construction of a U.S. Mint in Charlotte to strike the Carolina gold into coins. The building stood at the corner of Mint and West Trade streets until the 1930s, when it was taken down and reconstructed in the suburbs as the Mint Museum of Art—the state's first art museum.

World War I soldiers march down Tryon Street.

Shortly after the World War I armistice was signed, the Daughters of the American Revolution erected this monument honoring the soldiers of Camp Greene. It still stands at the corner of Wilkinson Boulevard and Monument Street.

The home of retailer William Henry Belk was designed by architect Charles C. Hook. The 1925 structure stands today at 120 Hawthorne Lane and is used by Presbyterian Hospital.

Businessman Osmond Barringer devised many publicity stunts, such as a 1919 promotion in which the young aviator seen second from left, Bennie Williams, became the first woman to pilot an airplane over Charlotte.

This dusty driver and mechanic pause during an open road race in front of the *Charlotte Observer* building on South Church Street in 1919. In the early days of the sport, mechanics often traveled along with the drivers, especially on long-distance races—their skills being needed to make repairs and often to put out fires.

Drivers line up for a photograph prior to the inaugural race at the Charlotte Speedway, October 25, 1924.

The Charlotte Speedway operated from October 1924 to September 1927. The one-and-a-quarter-mile oval track was constructed of pine and cypress planks and banked 40 degrees in the turns—significantly steeper than modern super speedways. Widely regarded as the fastest speedway in the world at the time, its high-banked turns allowed drivers to easily exceed 140 miles per hour and set numerous new world speed records.

One of many hotels that sprang up during the World War I era, Merton C. Propst's Clayton opened on the northwest corner of Church and Fifth streets. The European-style hotel—seen here around 1920—boasted 100 rooms and 50 baths, which rented at rates of $1 and $1.50. The Clayton was demolished in the mid-1970s.

Completed in 1923, Efird's department store wowed Charlotteans with its moving escalator—the only store south of Philadelphia with such a device. Louis Asbury designed the building; the J. A. Jones company erected it.

Officer Frank R. Ferguson keeps a dutiful eye on Charlotte's city streets (ca. 1920s).

Roland E. Ferguson worked for the Sanitary Steam Laundry, which offered pick-up and delivery service. Here he stands with his truck on North Cecil Street.

This 1920s parade float advertises a local tire manufacturer.

The aptly named Professional Building housed offices for numerous doctors, lawyers, and other small, independent businesses. Completed in 1924 by the J. A. Jones construction firm and designed by Louis Asbury, the building stood at North Tryon and Seventh streets.

Warehouses and freight cars along the Southern Railway at Park Avenue in 1931. Huttig—a national distributor of building products—actually closed its Charlotte operations two years before this image was recorded.

Albert Kahn, the famous industrial architect from Detroit, designed the Coddington Building, which once stood at Graham and Trade streets. C. C. Coddington, the Buick distributor for North and South Carolina in the mid-1920s, headquartered his operations here. For a while the building even housed the WBT radio station.

The U.S. Court House and Post Office—the fifth Mecklenburg County Courthouse—is located at 700 East Trade Street. Built at a cost of $1 million, it first opened in 1928.

Charlotte's booming economy did not benefit everyone. Poverty held many in its grip, and along with it came blight and decay in many parts of the city. Shown here is the W. A. Simerson Grocery on North Brevard Street (ca. 1948).

The beginning of the automobile age in the South created numerous opportunities for enterprising entrepreneurs to start their own businesses.

Completed in 1909, First Baptist Church was home to one of the most influential Christian congregations in the city and is one of the most distinctive works of eminent Charlotte architect James M. McMichael—who designed more than 1,000 houses of worship. The structure has Romanesque and Gothic elements, but the design is dominated by its central Byzantine dome. Though the congregation moved on to a new sanctuary, the structure has been preserved as a performing arts space.

Built in 1923, Central High School is located at Elizabeth Avenue and Kings Drive. Charlotte College—now UNC Charlotte—got its start offering night classes to returning GIs on the campus beginning in 1946. The school is now part of Central Piedmont Community College's central campus.

Charlotte's location along the Southern Railway made it an ideal location for warehousing and distribution.

Completed in 1928, this new bridge spanned the Catawba River.

The Y.M.C.A. moved to this location at 330 South Tryon Street in 1908 and is seen here in the mid-1920s. The location remained the Y's home until May 1960, when it moved to its present home on Morehead Street—known now as the Dowd Branch.

Charlotte Open Air School was an experiment based on the 1920s belief that cold air was beneficial for students. School Superintendent Harry P. Harding stands at the rear of the classroom.

WATCH CHARLOTTE GROW

In the mid-1920s, Hayes Bus Lines offered service between Charlotte and Columbia using standard passenger automobiles—one of which is seen here in front of the Firestone Tire and Rubber Company on Fifth Street.

In 1925, the Ford Motor Company opened a gigantic automobile assembly plant on Statesville Avenue. This facility—the third built in the city by the Detroit automobile manufacturer—assembled cars from components shipped down by railroad. Workers at the plant put together 130,000 Model T's and almost 100,000 Model A's for distribution in the Southeast. Production slowed greatly after the October 1929 stock market crash and ceased altogether in 1932.

East Trade Street at the corner of College Street, looking toward the Square (1920s).

In the 1930s, President Franklin D. Roosevelt called southern poverty the nation's "number one economic problem." To address that issue and to fight the nationwide Great Depression, Roosevelt (seen here during his 1936 visit to Charlotte) poured federal dollars into building projects here and all over America. This investment stepped up as the nation entered World War II and continued during the cold war. New military bases, hospitals, schools, and highways remade Charlotte.

New Deal workers completed Memorial Stadium in September 1936, just in time to host President Roosevelt. The president delivered a stirring speech, titled "Green Pastures," in which he proclaimed that the South could not prosper so long as the working people, especially the South's cotton farmers, could not make ends meet.

South Tryon, looking north from Fourth Street.

Shortly following Duke's conversion to motorbuses, the streetcar barn at the corner of South Boulevard and Bland Street was converted to meet the needs of the new transportation system. The number of buses operated by Duke Power grew from just 15 in 1937 to approximately 60 at the time of the 1938 changeover. The structure fell victim to Charlotte's hungry bulldozers in the summer of 2006.

Independence Square, showing the site of British general Cornwallis' headquarters during the American Revolution.

In white neighborhoods, barbershops were segregated, but ironically were usually owned and operated by African-Americans, such as this uptown shop. White barbers were rare in the South into the twentieth century.

Built in 1924 near the Southern Railway Station, the ten-story Hotel Charlotte once dominated the 200 block of West Trade Street. Its imposing edifice graced with terra cotta caps was designed by New York architect W. L. Stoddard. The hotel was also regional home to Victor Records, which recorded numerous stars from the golden age of country music—including Bill and Charlie Monroe and the Carter Family.

Around 1928, in the middle of a South Tryon skyscraper boom, several area litigators pooled their resources to erect the eight-story Lawyers Building at 307 South Tryon Street. The new structure was situated perfectly to allow its attorney tenants access to the new courthouse on East Trade.

Crowds filled the square for 1929's reunion of Confederate veterans.

South Tryon Street, facing north from the vicinity of First Street. The old Charlotte Observer building is visible at far-left. The spire of Saint Peter's Catholic Church is clearly visible at right.

Two women repair a plane at Charlotte's Morris Field during World War II.

Facing north on North Tryon Street.

Looking north up South Tryon Street's canyon of skyscrapers. Beginning in the late 1920s, South Tryon came to be seen as the city's financial district—akin to New York's Wall Street. South Tryon Street addresses were highly coveted by businesses wanting to be symbolically linked to this symbol of the city's power.

Mecklenburg County built its fifth courthouse on Trade Street in 1928.

Phillip Lance got his start roasting peanuts from a downtown cart in 1913. Three years later his wife, Nancy, and daughter Mary got the idea of spreading peanut butter on crackers—inventing the snack cracker! Today, Charlotte-based Lance is one of the South's biggest snack makers. Pictured are Lance employees.

The Lance plant on South Boulevard about 1946.

The southwest corner of Tryon and Third streets (ca. 1940).

East Seventh Street (ca. 1948).

Parishioners leave First Presbyterian Church.

Built so students from Alexander Graham Junior High could safely cross the street, this tunnel once connected South Boulevard to East Morehead Street. The Dowd Flats are visible in the background (ca. 1950).

Trade Street from Brevard facing Caldwell Avenue, as it appeared in the mid-1950s.

These businesses lined West First Street between Church and Mint in the early 1950s.

Designed by Frank P. Milburn and considered the finest office building in North Carolina at the time of its completion around 1898, the Piedmont Building stood as part of the canyon of skyscrapers that lined South Tryon Street until its demolition in 1956.

A crowd of more than 60,000 filled Freedom Park on May 20, 1954, to hear an address by President Dwight D. Eisenhower. The event was one of the grandest annual celebrations honoring the Mecklenburg Declaration of Independence. Earlier guests of honor had included Woodrow Wilson (1916), and William Howard Taft (1909). The last large celebration took place in 1975, when President Gerald Ford appeared.

Senator John F. Kennedy arriving at Douglas Airport in January 1959.

People at the Square (ca. 1950).

People at the Square (ca. 1955).

Only 968 Charlotteans had phone service when the Southern Bell Telephone and Telegraph Company purchased the Charlotte exchange in 1904. Bell moved operations to this building on Caldwell Street when the dial system came to Charlotte in 1929.

West on Trade Street, just past its intersection with Church (ca. 1950). The Selwyn Hotel is at right.

Building his way up from a job
as a manufacturer's agent, Jim
Turner founded National Welders
Supply Company in 1941 and set
up shop on South Tryon Street.
The fledgling enterprise would
grow to encompass multiple
service centers in four states.

Behind Jim Turner's leadership, National Welders grew well beyond the confines of the original Tryon Street storefront.

Turner's Welders Supply store openings headed south, as illustrated by this photo of the Florence, South Carolina, branch.

Among his many initiatives, Jim Turner of National Welders Supply Company established a low-cost school to train welders for work in the East Coast shipyards during World War II.

A parking lot behind City Hall (late 1950s).

STRENGTH AND RESOLVE

Sculptured by Georgian artist E. M. Viquesney, *Spirit of the American Doughboy* originally stood on the grounds of the old courthouse and was given in honor of the men from Mecklenburg County who valiantly served in World War I. Today the statue is seen on the northeast corner of Trade and Davidson streets.

Architect Frank Milburn designed Charlotte's Mediterranean-style passenger station for the Southern Railway, seen here from Depot Street in 1964. The building graced West Trade Street downtown and welcomed travelers to the city from 1905, until it was razed in the 1960s.

Seen here leaving the area north of the rail yard, the last passenger train departed the Southern Railway Station in November 1962.

A minor league baseball franchise, the Charlotte O's played during the late 1970s and early 1980s in Crockett Park on Dilworth's Magnolia Avenue. Renamed the Charlotte Knights, the team moved to a new stadium in Fort Mill, South Carolina, in 1987.

The sit-in movement began in Greensboro, North Carolina, in February 1960, when four well-dressed black students sat down at a whites-only lunch counter and refused to leave until they were served. Nine days later, students from Charlotte's Johnson C. Smith University picked up the idea. Led by J. Charles Jones, 200 students marched uptown and took over the Woolworth's counter as well as all the other lunch counters. After more than five months, the students prevailed and lunch counters began serving African-Americans.

Charlotte dentist and Presbyterian minister Reginald Hawkins (right) with Martin Luther King, Jr., at Johnson C. Smith University in 1966. Throughout the 1960s, Hawkins led protests and filed lawsuits that resulted in the desegregation of Charlotte Memorial Hospital, Mercy Hospital, the North Carolina Dental Society, and the Charlotte Y.M.C.A.

Seen here after winning the pole for the 1961 World 600 in Charlotte, Richard Petty dominated the sport of auto-racing in the 1960s. His best year was 1967, when he won 27 of 48 races—including a record 10 in a row—finished second place 7 times, and easily cruised to the championship.

Beginning in 1953, WBTV aired a popular noontime show for women starring Betty Feezor. Feezor hosted her own show at a time when very few women held such roles.

The Wachovia Building on South Tryon Street (ca. 1961). Charlotte-based First Union acquired its Winston-Salem-based rival in 2001. The corporation—now the fifth-largest bank in the United States—took the Wachovia name and kept its headquarters in Charlotte.

Pushed to success under the leadership of Bonnie Cone, Charlotte College soon outgrew its home in Central High School, as well as a building erected on Cecil Street. In 1959, the school began to acquire land for its current site on Highway 49, becoming a four-year institution in 1963. Two years later the school became the fourth campus of the University of North Carolina, known since as UNC Charlotte.

The first structure erected on the University of North Carolina's new suburban campus was the Kennedy Building, which housed everything from the chancellor's office to the library.

In 1927, the U.S. Federal Reserve chose Charlotte as the site for its branch serving the Carolinas. The Federal Reserve bridges banks with the federal government—putting new dollar bills in circulation and shredding old ones. It also "clears" checks—returns a check written anywhere in the Carolinas back to its home bank. Fast access to "the Fed" gave Charlotte banks advantages over banks farther away. Shown here is an employee clearing checks in the 1970s.

Professional hockey came to Charlotte after a 1956 fire displaced the Baltimore Clippers. Expecting a lackluster response in the South, the team drew an initial crowd of over 10,000—3,000 had to be turned away. Charlotteans discovered a love for this violent "northern" sport. Rechristened the Charlotte Checkers, the team won the 1974 Southern Hockey League championship and played until 1977. The current Charlotte Checkers team was established in 1993 as an affiliate of the NHL's New York Rangers.

Segregation protest in progress.

In 1973, activists in the Charlotte women's movement established a chapter of the National Organization for Women. Despite being a small group, when compared with bigger cities, Charlotte NOW effected a great deal of change. Shown here are volunteers in Latta Park in 1975.

The Carolina piedmont has been basketball-mad dating back to textile mill teams and such fierce college rivalries as Winston-Salem State versus Johnson C. Smith, and Chapel Hill versus Duke. In 1988, pro ball arrived. The NBA Charlotte Hornets played to sell-out crowds. The Sting, of the Women's National Basketball Association, soon joined them. A new NBA team, the Bobcats, began playing in 2004 after the Hornets moved to New Orleans. The Bobcats are owned by Robert Johnson, billionaire founder of BET, the Black Entertainment Television channel. Here, Tyrone "Muggsy" Bogues scores against the Miami Heat in 1988.

Built between 1938 and 1940 with federal money as part of Roosevelt's New Deal, Charlotte Memorial Hospital was originally four stories tall with just 300 beds. The hospital was instrumental in dealing with the polio epidemic that swept through the Carolinas in 1948. The complex—seen here in 1961—has expanded several times over the years and now serves the community as a Medical Center.

Charlotte's Masonic Lodge enlisted architects Charles Christian Hook and Willard Rogers to design its ornate Egyptian Revival–style temple. The J. A. Jones construction company erected the structure, which opened in 1914. The building—pictured here in the mid-1920s—burned in the late 1930s, but was quickly rebuilt according to the original plans. The temple stood among the canyon of skyscrapers that lined South Tryon Street, until it was purchased and demolished by First Union in the late 1980s. It was the last example of Egyptian Revival architecture in North Carolina.

Notes on the Photographs

These notes, listed by page number, attempt to include all aspects known of the photographs. Each of the photographs is identified by the page number, a title or description, photographer and collection, archive, and call or box number when applicable. Although every attempt was made to collect all data, in some cases complete data may have been unavailable due to the age and condition of some of the photographs and records.

Printed in the USA
CPSIA information can be obtained
at www.ICGtesting.com
JSHW051012181023
50422JS00020B/83